Overcoming the Odds

Bo Jackson

Jon Kramer

RSVP

RAINTREE STECK-VAUGHN
PUBLISHERS
The Steck-Vaughn Company

Austin, Texas

Published by Raintree Steck-Vaughn Publishers,
an imprint of Steck-Vaughn Company

Developed for Steck-Vaughn Company by
Visual Education Corporation, Princeton, New Jersey
Project Director: Paula McGuire
Editor: Marilyn Miller
Photo Research: Marty Levick
Electronic Preparation: Cynthia C. Feldner
Production Supervisor: Barbara A. Kopel
Electronic Production: Maxson Crandall, Lisa Evans-Skopas
Interior Design: Maxson Crandall

Raintree Steck-Vaughn Publishers staff
Editor: Helene Resky
Project Manager: Joyce Spicer

Photo Credits: **Cover (left):** © Paul Spinelli/NFL PHOTOS; **Cover (right):** © Focus On
Sports; **7:** Chuck Solomon; **9:** © Joe McNally/*Sports Illustrated;* **10:** The Birmingham
News Company; **13:** Auburn University; **15:** Auburn University; **17:** Auburn University;
19: Auburn University; **21:** Rich Addicks; **23:** © Focus On Sports; **25:** © Paul
Spinelli/NFL PHOTOS; **28:** © Focus On Sports; **31:** © Focus On Sports; **34:** Steven
Dunn/ALLSPORT USA; **36:** Wide World Photos, Inc.; **37:** Wide World Photos, Inc.;
38: © Focus On Sports; **40:** © Paul Spinelli/NFL PHOTOS; **41:** Wide World Photos, Inc.

Library of Congress Cataloging-in-Publication Data
Kramer, Jon.
    Bo Jackson / Jon Kramer.
        p.   cm. — (Overcoming the odds)
    Includes bibliographical references (p.   ) and index.
    Summary: A biography of the football player with the Los Angeles Raiders who de-
voted himself to baseball after a serious injury ended his football career.
    ISBN 0-8172-4123-X
    1. Jackson, Bo, 1962- — Juvenile literature.   2. Baseball players — United States —
Biography — Juvenile literature.   3. Football players — United States — Biography —
Juvenile literature.   [1. Jackson, Bo, 1962- .   2. Football players.   3. Baseball players.
4. Afro-Americans — Biography.]   I. Title.   II. Series.
GV865.J28K73   1996
796.357′092—dc20
[B]   95-46213
                                                                                           CIP
                                                                                            AC

Printed and bound in the United States
1 2 3 4 5 6 7 8 9 0   99 98 97 96 95

Table of contents

Chapter 1

Bo Knows Comebacks

Hollywood could not have written a better script. He was a gifted athlete whose combination of power and speed left rivals in awe: a man good enough to play in baseball's All-Star Game; a man who became one of football's best running backs; a man so famous that people knew him by just two letters—Bo.

He was born Vincent Edward Jackson, but everyone called him Bo. He got the nickname at age six while growing up in Alabama. Now, 24 years later, he was trying to stage a comeback.

Bo had suffered a hip injury while playing football for the Los Angeles Raiders. He was injured in a play-off game against the Cincinnati Bengals on January 13, 1991. The injury was so bad it ended his football career.

Bo still hoped to play baseball. After the Kansas City Royals allowed him to become a free agent, he signed with the Chicago White Sox. Bo missed almost all of the 1991 baseball season. He went to

Bo Jackson's remarkable talent and competitive spirit made him an All-Star in both baseball and football.

spring training in 1992. But the injured hip was not responding to treatment. An operation was his only hope.

On April 5, 1992, Bo's hip was replaced with an artificial one. The surgery is more common in older people. It is very rarely done on a world-class athlete. Few people ever expected Bo to return to baseball.

Bo had enough money to live on for the rest of his life. Did he really need to continue his athletic career? Fans knew he had reached the top in both baseball and football. Wasn't the most important thing to be able to walk normally?

Bo told everyone he'd be back. He worked long and hard in the Sox training room. He even moved to Phoenix to work with a special trainer. When 1993 came around, Bo was ready to make history.

On April 9, the White Sox played their home opener against the New York Yankees. The fans cheered when Bo stepped to the plate as a pinch hitter. It was his first at-bat of the season.

Bo slugged Neal Heaton's first pitch over the right-field wall. The fans at Comiskey Park went crazy! Bo had hit a home run in his first swing of the season! His comeback was complete. Teammate Frank Thomas said that it was like a fairy tale.

Bo hit 16 homers that year, including a three-run blast on September 27. This hit clinched the division title for the White Sox. Chicago was in the play-offs for the first time in ten years. No wonder

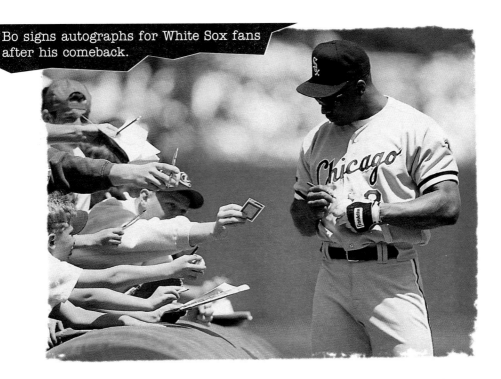

Bo signs autographs for White Sox fans after his comeback.

The Sporting News named Bo Comeback Player of the Year.

"I've never seen anyone rehab like Bo did," said Sox clubhouse-man Willie Thompson. "The program he went through was torture."

Before Bo's comeback season began, the Sox pitching coach, Walt Hriniak, was watching Bo in the batting cage during spring training. "I was thinking, 'What's Bo doing here? He's got an artificial hip. What's he trying to do? He can't hit major league pitching,'" said Hriniak.

A second later, Bo began belting balls over the fence. "He convinced me plenty that he could still hit," said Hriniak.

Chapter 2

Alabama Roots

Vincent Edward Jackson was born on November 30, 1962, in Bessemer, Alabama, a town near Birmingham. Young Vincent was the eighth of ten children. His mother, Florence Jackson, worked as a motel housekeeper.

Vincent's father was A.D. Adams, a local steelworker. He lived on the other side of town, away from Florence and the children. A.D. and Florence were not married. A.D. would often go months without seeing his son.

Vincent was an active little boy. By the age of six, he was being called "Bo'-hog." That's a Southern term for a boar, which is a wild, nasty pig. Later, the name was shortened to "Bo." That's what he's been called ever since.

Bo wasn't very nice growing up. "You name it, I did it," he said. Bo broke windows, beat up kids, and stole bikes. He was especially known for his rock throwing. "I was a bully," said Bo.

Bo had trouble speaking when he was young. He stuttered, and people made fun of him. Some even

Bo's brothers and sisters are some of his biggest fans.

called him stupid. Bo was hurt by comments like that. He became angry and withdrawn.

Florence Jackson tried to control her son. She told Bo that he'd end up in jail if he didn't change his ways. His brother even mentioned reform school. Bo finally got the message when he was 13.

One summer day, Bo and some friends decided to go swimming. On their way to the lake, they walked past a hog pen owned by a Baptist minister. They stopped and threw some rocks. By the time they were done, $3,000 worth of pigs were dead.

Bo's mother was furious. She told the minister she couldn't control her son. If the minister wanted to send Bo to reform school, that was okay with her.

Bo knew he had to change if he didn't want to end up in reform school. He and his friends took jobs to help pay for the pigs that they had killed.

Bo later told a writer that this was when he knew he had to straighten up. He realized that he could be sent to jail for some of the things that he was doing.

Bo decided to apply his talents to sports. As a ninth grader, he made the track team at McAdory High School. Bo ran the hurdles and learned the high jump. He was so good that his coach suggested he try the decathlon. The decathlon is a series of ten events, consisting of running, jumping, and throwing. It's an event only the best athletes can enter.

Bo won Alabama's high school decathlon in his junior and senior years. He was the state champ in the triple jump. Bo also set a state record in the 100-yard dash. He ran it in 9.54 seconds!

Bo felt that he changed in high school. He was no longer "that bad Jackson kid." Now he didn't look for trouble. He helped around the house before school and then went to practice. Afterward, he went home and studied. His favorite subjects were science, English, and math.

Bo knew he wanted to go to college. He wanted to be an engineer or a pilot. Bo was crazy about airplanes. He would watch them rise in the sky and then disappear beyond the horizon. He wondered where they went.

Bo began thinking that maybe there was a world beyond the horizon. He became more and more sure that playing ball was going to help him get there.

During the fall, Bo turned his attention to football. He made McAdory's football team as a tenth grader. Bo played fullback on offense and end on defense. He also did the placekicking. That's attempting to kick the ball through the goalposts to score a point after touchdown (PAT) or a field goal. A PAT is one point. A field goal is three points.

Bo's mother didn't like football. She was afraid Bo would get hurt playing. That's why she didn't go to any of the games. It wasn't Bo's favorite sport either. He played it mostly to pass the time after baseball season. Football was a kind of hobby.

It was some hobby! Bo scored 29 points in one game during his junior season. He ran for three touchdowns and caught a pass for another touchdown. Bo also booted a field goal and kicked a pair of extra points.

Bo averaged more than ten yards a carry as a senior. He scored 17 touchdowns and was named All-State. Bo was also a terror on defense. In one game, Bo tackled the quarterback just after he had thrown a pass. Then Bo scrambled to his feet and tackled the receiver!

Bo was also a natural baseball player. He batted .450 as a junior and had a 9–1 record as a pitcher. His performance was not bad for someone who couldn't practice a lot because of the time he spent on other sports. Bo's track meets were often scheduled for the same time as his baseball games. He simply chose to be in the more important event.

Bo hit .493 as a senior. He played center field or shortstop. He also tied a national high school record by belting 20 home runs in 25 games. Bo remembers stealing about 90 bases during his high school career. He thinks he was thrown out only once.

Bo's fastball was clocked at 92 miles per hour. That's major league speed! He even pitched two no-hitters during high school. Bo had lots of success, but pitching bored him. He hated that there was not enough action.

Dozens of major league scouts came to see Bo play. The New York Yankees drafted him after his senior year in 1982. The Yankees offered him $250,000 to sign. Bo asked his mother what to do. She told him to go to college. Money was something that Bo could have for a short time. But he would have education for his whole life.

The Jacksons refused the Yankees' offer. Bo said that saying "no" was easy. He had been poor all his life. How could he miss something he never had? Bo felt sure that the money would be there later in his life.

Several schools offered football scholarships. Bo knew that he wanted to stay as close as possible to his home and family. He had traveled outside of Alabama only once.

Two schools really turned up the heat. The University of Alabama and Auburn University are bitter rivals in the state. Both are known for having tremendous football programs. And both of them wanted the young man from Bessemer.

Auburn won the battle. Its location in the southeastern part of Alabama, only 100 miles (160 km) from Bo's hometown, made the difference. Pat Dye was the Tigers' football coach. He told Bo he could join the baseball and track teams in the spring. That decided it! Bo enrolled at Auburn in the fall of 1982.

Despite offers from several schools to play football, Bo chose nearby Auburn, where he also participated in baseball and track.

Chapter 3

Heisman Trophy Winner

Bo was very lonely in his early days at Auburn. Practices were long and hard. The weather was hot. The coaches were tough. It was also the first time he had been away from his family. Soon after the season started, Bo decided enough was enough.

He gathered his clothes and went to the bus station in nearby Opelika, Alabama. Before buying a ticket, Bo stopped to think. He knew how disappointed his mother would be if he quit school. She was proud of him. So were his brothers and sisters. What would they think if he quit?

Bo also wondered what he would do with his life. If he went home, Bo knew that he would just hang around. But he didn't want to do nothing at all like other guys he had seen. Bo didn't want to be a nobody. He felt that he wanted to do something with his life.

Bo never bought that ticket. He returned to Auburn. It was soon clear that Bo had made the right decision. He scored nine touchdowns and

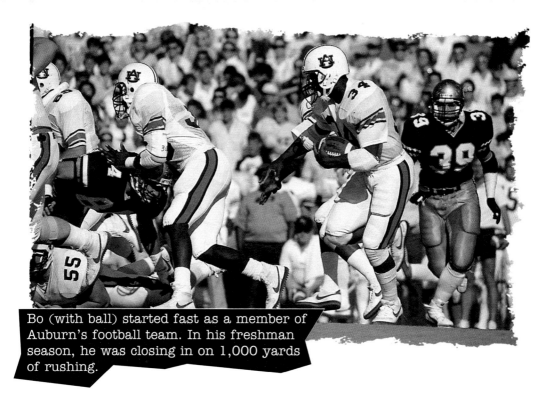

Bo (with ball) started fast as a member of Auburn's football team. In his freshman season, he was closing in on 1,000 yards of rushing.

rushed for 829 yards as a freshman. Bo even scored the winning touchdown in the Tigers' game against their big rival Alabama.

A few weeks later, Bo helped Auburn win the Tangerine Bowl against Boston College. He ran track the rest of the winter. Then he switched to baseball in the spring. Bo became the first Auburn athlete to make the school teams in all three sports in 30 years!

Baseball was a real struggle. Bo struck out in each of his first 21 at-bats. He refused to quit. By the end of the season, his batting average was .279.

Bo loved baseball. But he was one of the best college football players in the nation. As a sophomore in 1983, he rushed for 1,213 yards. He scored 12 touchdowns. Auburn lost only one game that season. The team went on to defeat Michigan in the Sugar Bowl. Bo ran for 130 yards that night to cap a great season.

Bo decided to skip baseball in 1984. He hoped to qualify for the Olympics as a sprinter. A sprinter is a runner who races short distances. Bo dreamed about racing the great American runner Carl Lewis for the gold medal. Bo worked hard, but he just couldn't make the U.S. team.

That was a major setback. He faced another setback several months later, in the second game of the football season. Bo fell hard while running against Texas and separated his shoulder. He missed six games of his junior season. Bo returned for the last four games and quickly showed everyone he was as good as new. He was named Most Valuable Player (MVP) of the Liberty Bowl after scoring two touchdowns.

Auburn coach Pat Dye was impressed. He said that Bo was not just another athlete. Bo was more like a guy from another planet!

Bo was determined to get a good education at Auburn. He studied psychology. Then he switched to family and child development as a junior. It made a great impression on him that his mother had raised all her children by herself.

Bo has always loved kids. In college he worked with youngsters at the Auburn Child Study Center. There, he met a young woman named Linda Garrett.

Linda was studying psychology in college. Bo and Linda studied together at her apartment. At first, the two were just friends. Then they fell in love, and in September 1987, they got married. Linda is one of the few people who calls Bo by his given name of Vincent.

Bo learned responsibility in college. Some days he opened a book and said, "I can't do this, I got a headache." Then a little bell rang in his head, and he would say, "I got to."

It's amazing that Bo had time to study. He came into his own as a baseball player during his junior year. Bo hit .401 that season. He had 17 homers and 43 runs batted in (RBIs) in 42 games.

Bo's baseball skills really came together in his junior year at Auburn. That season he batted over .400.

After his junior year, Bo was once again eligible for the major league draft. The California Angels selected him, but Bo refused to sign. He wanted to play one more season of football.

Bo also enjoyed his time away from the field. He liked going to class like other students and not standing out. Bo liked taking notes and asking questions. He enjoyed learning.

Bo began his senior season as one of the leading contenders for the Heisman Trophy. That's an award given to the best college football player in the country. Many great players have won it when they were in college, like Barry Sanders (Oklahoma State), Herschel Walker (University of Virginia), and Marcus Allen (University of Southern California).

Bo gained 290 yards in the opening game of 1985. He never looked back. Despite some injuries, Bo ran for 1,786 yards that season. He also scored 17 touchdowns. Bo had become Auburn's all-time leader in both running and touchdowns scored. The proudest moment of his amateur career came when he won the Heisman Trophy in December.

Bo accepted the award at the Downtown Athletic Club in New York City. The other finalists were Miami's Vinny Testaverde, Iowa's Chuck Long, and Michigan State's Lorenzo White. All three went on to play professional football.

When Bo was announced as the winner, his heart started to pound. He gave a short speech. Then he

Bo accepts the 1985 Heisman Trophy.

called his mother in Alabama. His family and the entire neighborhood were having a party. It went on through the night.

A few days later, Bo was honored at the Heisman dinner. He had to give another speech. Bo decided to send a message to his young fans. He told them to set the highest goals possible and not stop until they achieved them.

Bo had to play one more football game for Auburn. It was the 1986 Cotton Bowl in Dallas, Texas. Bo gained 129 yards that day. But Auburn lost to Texas A&M. It was the only bowl game Auburn lost during Bo's college career.

Now it was time for a little fun. Bo flew to Japan to play in a college All-Star game. It was his first trip overseas. A week later, he played in another All-Star game. That event was held a little closer to home in Mobile, Alabama.

Bo was under a lot of pressure. Everyone wanted to know which sport he was going to play as a professional. The National Football League's (NFL) Tampa Bay Buccaneers drafted Bo first overall in April 1986. They expected him to turn the team around. Two months later, the Kansas City Royals chose Bo in the fourth round of the baseball draft.

Bo told everyone that he was not going to decide until June. First, he had to finish his senior year of college.

But Bo did tell Tampa Bay and Kansas City to make their best offers. The Buccaneers offered him a minimum of $2 million a year. He would probably earn more than $4 million over five years. The Royals guaranteed him $200,000 a year. They said he could earn $1 million over three years.

In addition, the Nike shoe company wanted to sign Bo to a contract. They agreed to pay him more money if he chose football. It looked like a simple decision.

"Money isn't the main thing," Bo kept saying. "Money can't buy happiness, and Bo Jackson wants to be happy."

Bo poses as Super Bo for a special college football section of a local newspaper, the *Atlanta Journal*, during his last year at Auburn.

Chapter 4

Kansas City, Here I Come

Bo reviewed his choices. He then flew to California to visit Reggie Jackson. The two Jacksons are not related. Bo had met Reggie a few months earlier at a dinner. Reggie was one of baseball's biggest stars. He hit more than 500 home runs in his career and made it into the Baseball Hall of Fame. He was known as "Mr. October" because he had so much success in the World Series.

Reggie had also played two sports growing up. He actually had gone to college on a football scholarship. Reggie told Bo he could have a longer career in baseball. Over time, he could make more money in the sport. Reggie also said there was a greater risk of injury in football.

Bo went back to Alabama and made his decision. He would sign with Kansas City. "My first love is baseball," he said. "I went with what's in my heart."

"In life you take chances," he added. "My goal is to be the best baseball player Bo Jackson can be. My strengths are my speed and my arm. I need to work on hitting the curveball."

Bo was not ready to play in the major leagues. He needed to get some experience in the minors. The Royals sent him to their minor league team in Memphis, Tennessee.

Bo started slowly. He had only four hits in his first 45 at-bats. Bo dropped balls in the outfield. He also got picked off bases. People wondered if he should give up and return to football.

Bo played with the Kansas City Royals' minor league team, the Memphis Chicks, for part of the 1986 season.

During the season, things gradually changed. Bo raised his average to .277. The Royals decided that he was ready to play for them. He spent the rest of 1986 in Kansas City. Facing big-league pitching for the first time, Bo hit .207. He had two home runs and nine RBIs in 25 games.

After the season, Bo returned to Auburn. There, he ran with the Tigers' track team. Bo also worked out with the baseball squad.

The Royals wanted Bo to work on his fielding. Eddie Napoleon worked with him. Napoleon was a Royals instructor who became a close friend. He and Bo spent a lot of time together.

"Bo had spent so little time playing baseball," Napoleon said. "He didn't even know how to hold his glove to field ground balls. But he worked, and he listened. Because he's such a great athlete, he learned fast."

Bo worked hard that winter. It paid off when he was named the Royals' starting left fielder in 1987. Bo still struck out a lot, but he also displayed great power. By midseason, he was leading the team in homers (18) and RBIs (45).

Lots of people were impressed. Detroit Tigers manager Sparky Anderson said that Bo was the best athlete he had ever seen playing baseball.

Royals teammate Willie Wilson also talked about Bo. Wilson said that Bo could hit a grounder to third base and still make it safely to first base.

At the end of his first season as a major leaguer, Bo surprised everyone. He announced that he was joining the Los Angeles Raiders as a running back.

Then at his next at-bat, he could hit a tremendous home run.

But on July 11, 1987, Bo shocked everyone in Kansas City. He said that he was joining the NFL's Los Angeles Raiders at the end of the baseball season. The Tampa Bay Buccaneers had lost their rights to Bo when they couldn't sign him. The Raiders had taken a gamble. They had picked him in the seventh round of the 1987 NFL draft.

Bo said that the Kansas City Royals still came first. Whatever happened after the baseball season was a hobby.

But Royals fans were upset. They called Bo a traitor. The fact that he was joining the Raiders made it worse. The Raiders were bitter football rivals of the Kansas City Chiefs. Many experts felt Bo had made a huge mistake. They said he couldn't play the two sports at such a high level. No athlete had ever done this before.

Bo felt that he had nothing to prove. In college he had shown that he could play football. In Kansas City he had proved that he could play major league baseball. His decision also didn't have to do with money. Bo wanted to have fun. Playing football and baseball seemed like fun!

Many people started to compare Bo to Jim Thorpe. Thorpe was a legendary athlete who had become a Hall-of-Fame football player. He also had played pro baseball, without great success. A movie had been made about his life.

John Elway had also tried minor league baseball before deciding to stick with football. And Danny Ainge had struggled with baseball before beginning his long career with the National Basketball Association (NBA).

Bo wanted to do what these other athletes could not. After belting 22 homers for the Royals, he joined the Raiders in October. He said that if most people didn't think he could, he would try to prove them wrong every time! Bo made his NFL debut on November 1, 1987, against the New England Patriots. The Raiders lost the first four games that he played in. Things looked bad when they flew to Seattle to meet the Seahawks on November 30.

The game against the Seahawks was played on Bo's 25th birthday. It was televised on "Monday Night Football." Bo had started slowly with the Raiders. Now he was ready to break out.

Bo caught an early touchdown pass. Then he ran 91 yards for another score. Bo took a pitchout, cut outside, and flew past several defenders. His 91-yard run was the longest in Raiders history. He didn't stop running until he was halfway up the locker-room tunnel.

Bo rushed for 221 yards that night to set a club record. He scored another touchdown in the third quarter. That gave him three for the game. The Raiders won 37–14 to break a seven-game losing streak.

Bo had put on a tremendous show. It was one of the greatest ever on "Monday Night Football." He was becoming a real star in both his sports!

Raiders defensive tackle Howie Long was impressed. He got chills watching Bo. Everyone Long talked to said that Bo was the best runner they had ever seen.

Bo rushed for 554 yards in 1987. His average of 6.8 yards per carry was outstanding. Bo also caught 16 passes for 136 yards and two touchdowns. And he only played seven games! No wonder he was named Rookie of the Year by several football publications.

The football season ended in January. In March, it was time for baseball again. Bo felt he had a lot to prove in 1988. Like many young players, Bo was striving for consistency.

Bo scores a touchdown in a 1987 game between the Raiders and the Buffalo Bills.

Bo missed a month of baseball because of a torn hamstring. He still posted solid numbers in 1988. Bo became the first player in Royals history to hit 25 homers and steal 25 bases in the same season. He was also becoming a force in the outfield. Bo threw out 11 runners.

Milwaukee Brewer Paul Molitor said that Bo had so many ways to beat another club that it was frightening. Bo could hit home runs. He could steal bases. Bo would always find a way to win.

When the baseball season ended, Bo took ten days off before reporting to the Raiders. His first game was back in Kansas City against the Chiefs. The same fans who cheered Bo during the summer now rooted against him.

Bo did his best to silence them. He rushed for 70 yards and scored a touchdown to lead the Raiders to a 27–17 win. It was a good start. But the Raiders had their troubles in 1988. Bo rushed for 580 yards, yet the team finished with a 7–9 record. The Raiders missed the play-offs for the third straight season.

Chapter 5

A Home Run to Remember

By 1989, Bo had become one of America's most popular athletes. His biggest moment that year came in baseball's All-Star Game. It took place in Anaheim Stadium, home of the California Angels.

Bo was making his first All-Star appearance. He had received more votes than any other player in the American League. It was a chance to display his talents on baseball's biggest stage. Millions of people would be watching the game on television.

Bo led off the first inning against Rick Reuschel of the San Francisco Giants. He smashed Reuschel's second pitch 448 feet over the center-field wall! National League manager Tom Lasorda of the Los Angeles Dodgers was awed. He said that the ball Bo hit sounded like a golf ball!

Only four other players had ever hit a home run to lead off an All-Star Game. All of them—Frankie Frisch (1934), Lou Boudreau (1942), Willie Mays (1965), and Joe Morgan (1977)—made it into the Baseball Hall of Fame. Bo also became the ninth player to homer in his first All-Star at-bat.

In the second inning, Bo knocked in another run and stole a base. He became just the second player to hit a home run and steal a base in the same All-Star Game. Hall-of-Famer Willie Mays had been the first. It was easy to see why Bo was named Most Valuable Player (MVP) of the game.

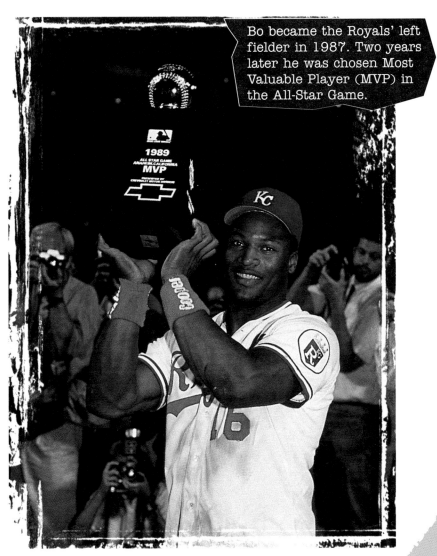

Bo became the Royals' left fielder in 1987. Two years later he was chosen Most Valuable Player (MVP) in the All-Star Game.

Lasorda said that Bo was the first player since Mickey Mantle to combine power with speed. Minnesota Twins star Kirby Puckett told Bo that he was his new idol.

That performance highlighted a great season. Bo set career highs in home runs (32), RBIs (105), and runs scored (86) in 1989. He ranked among the American League leaders in all three categories.

Bo took a short break. Then he joined the Raiders a month into the 1989 season. His best game was on November 5 against the Cincinnati Bengals. Bo scored on a 92-yard run to break the Raider record he had set in 1987. In all, he rushed for 159 yards—126 in the first half. He also scored two touchdowns.

Boomer Esiason was the Bengals' quarterback at the time. He said that Bo was possibly the best American athlete in the past 50 years.

Bo finished with a career-high 950 yards rushing in 1989. Not bad for someone who played only 11 of the Raiders' 16 games!

Raiders linebacker Linden King said that Bo was the fastest and strongest player he had ever seen. "When God was handing out talent, Bo got it all."

Raiders quarterback Vince Evans agreed. He said that as a running back, Bo had an amazing combination of speed, power, and grace.

Bo was just as successful off the field. Companies such as Nike, AT&T, and Pepsi lined up to do business with him. He earned a large amount of money doing commercials. Bo's most famous commercial was for the Nike shoe company. The popular spot featured Bo, hockey's Wayne Gretzky, basketball's Michael Jordan, and rock and roller Bo Diddley.

Bo had his best two-sports year in 1989. The next year Bo injured his shoulder playing against the Yankees. The injury caused him to miss a month of the baseball season.

But Bo still racked up 28 homers and 78 RBIs in 111 games. He was the first player in Royals history to hit at least 25 home runs for three straight years.

Teammate George Brett felt that Bo was awesome. Brett said that he would give anything to be in Bo's body for one day. Brett added that it was amazing to see Bo play at his best.

Bo made spectacular plays almost every day. He hit the longest home runs in the majors. Fans came to the park early just to watch him take batting practice.

In the field, Bo was out of this world. He made one running catch that made all the television highlights. It took place in Kansas City. Sprinting like a deer, Bo grabbed a long fly ball near the left-field wall. With only a few feet to stop, he ended up climbing the wall like Spiderman. Another time, he threw a runner out at home plate from the edge of the outfield track!

Even his strikeouts were exciting. When Bo got mad, he'd snap the bat over his leg like a twig. Were his thighs made of steel? It sure looked that way.

That fall was Bo's fourth season with the Raiders. He rushed for 698 yards and five touchdowns. He was also named to the Pro Bowl. That's football's version of the All-Star Game. It's held every year in Hawaii.

Bo never got a chance to play in that game. He had led the Raiders into the play-offs. Then he was injured in the club's first postseason game against Cincinnati. Bo hurt his hip when he was tackled after a long run. The injury did not simply end his season. It also ended his football career.

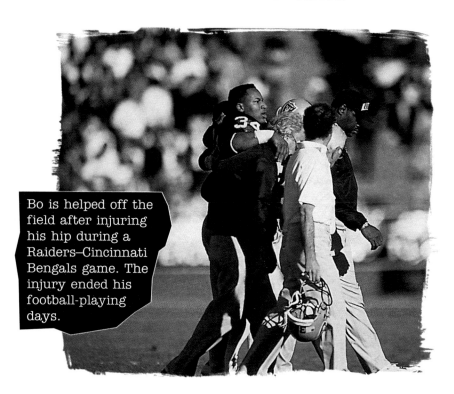

Bo is helped off the field after injuring his hip during a Raiders–Cincinnati Bengals game. The injury ended his football-playing days.

Chapter 6

The Road Back

Despite his injury, Bo was determined to play baseball again. He was still on crutches when he reported for spring training with the Royals in 1991. Kansas City did not know if Bo could ever play again. So the management decided to release him. The Chicago White Sox signed Bo two weeks later.

Bo missed almost all of the 1991 baseball season. He played a little in September, but things were not right. Power hitters use their legs to help drive the ball out of the park. Bo had trouble pushing off. He could barely run and could only swing with his arms. An operation was the only way to save his baseball career.

During spring training in 1992, Bo was a shadow of his former self. It was almost painful to watch. He ran with a limp and could not hit with any power. It looked like Bo was finished at the age of 29. Having an operation was the only way he could save his baseball career. It was a long shot.

After receiving an artificial hip, Bo missed all of the 1992 season. He worked around the clock to get back in shape. In Phoenix, Arizona, Bo met a trainer named Mack Newton. Newton had had his own hip replaced a few years earlier. He pushed Bo for hours at a time. Each workout was tougher than the last. A lesser man would have given up.

The best athletes have an inner drive to succeed. When people said he was wasting his time, Bo worked that much harder. He knew he'd never play football again. But baseball was his first love. He wasn't ready to give it up without a fight.

Bo holds on to his crutches as he waits to tape a Nike commercial in 1991.

Very few people ever expected him to return. But he did return, and in grand style, too. Bo hit a home run in his first at-bat of 1993! Nothing could be more dramatic. After the game, Bo said, "I never doubted myself."

Bo played 85 games for the White Sox that year. In July, he showed he was all the way back. In a game against the Seattle Mariners, Bo crushed a 472-foot home run. It was the longest that season by a White Sox player.

Bo's batting average (.232) was a little low. But he finished strong. In his last 11 games, he hit .306, with three homers, three doubles, and eight RBIs.

After the 1993 season, Bo's contract with the White Sox ended. He became a free agent. The California Angels signed him for the 1994 season. Bo was happy to have a chance to play in the Angels' ball club. He had spent his football career with the Los Angeles Raiders. His home was only an hour up the road from Anaheim Stadium, the Angels' ballpark.

It was also the Angels that had drafted Bo after his junior year at Auburn. In 1985, he had turned them down to play another season of football. And who could forget Bo's huge home run in the 1989 All-Star Game? It was hit in Anaheim Stadium.

Bo hit .279 in 1994 for the Angels. It was the highest batting average of his career. He smashed 13 homers and drove in 43 runs in just 201 at-bats. They were good numbers for a shortened season. On August 12 of that year, the players went on strike. The season was canceled in September. No World Series was played for the first time in 90 years.

Bo had a great first season with the California Angels in 1994. Too bad the season was cut short by the baseball strike!

Chapter 7

Away from the Field

Bo likes to hunt, fish, and be with his family in his spare time. He and his wife Linda have three children. Their boys are named Garrett and Nicholas. Their daughter's name is Morgan. She's the youngest.

George Brett says that Bo is a family man. His wife and his children are the most important things to him in the world.

Bo admires his wife very much. He says that Linda is his better half. "She's always there for me, always warm, always comforting. I can talk to her about anything."

Bo calls Linda a lot when he's on the road. He calls her in the morning when he gets up. He calls her before he goes to the ballpark. And he calls her after the game. Sometimes he even calls between innings.

The life of a famous athlete is not as easy as it looks. It's difficult for Bo to go out in public. People recognize him and ask for autographs. They even ask when he's trying to enjoy a day with his kids or when he's out in public eating.

Bo is a real family man. Here, he and his young son watch the Raiders from the sidelines.

Bo likes signing autographs if asked politely. He doesn't like it when people shout his name loudly or demand he sign. Bo thinks the best time for autographs is at the ballpark. Those are his business hours. He refuses to sign autographs when he's with his family. That is their time.

Bo is tough on the outside but soft on the inside. He has one of the biggest hearts around. Bo spends many hours on children's charities. He's active with groups such as the Make-A-Wish Foundation. The foundation grants wishes to dying children.

Linda Jackson says that children don't see Bo as a superstar. They see him as someone who cares about them. They don't talk about his great plays. They talk about how he plays with them.

When Bo visits sick children, he tries to make them smile. That makes him feel better than hitting a home run. It makes Bo feel like he's done something very important.

Bo outdid himself in 1990. On July 17, he had one of his greatest games in front of a sick teenager named Brian Newton. The place was New York's Yankee Stadium. The Newtons were from Chillicothe, Ohio. Thirteen-year-old Brian had come with his parents and younger sister, Brooke.

Brian was sick with cancer. His one wish was to meet Bo and Yankee first baseman Don Mattingly. Brian was to meet Bo before the game.

Bo signed a bunch of baseball cards for his young fan. He then asked Brian where he'd be sitting. Bo said he would try to wave to Brian during the game.

What followed was simply magical. Bo stepped to the plate in the first inning. George Brett was on first base with two men out. The count was two and two. Yankee pitcher Andy Hawkins threw a fastball. Bo hit a home run over the center-field fence. Brian didn't believe it. He had just met Bo, and here he was hitting a home run.

Two innings later, Bo came up again. Brett was on base. This time it took only one pitch. Bo ripped a Hawkins fastball 464 feet (140 km)! It was another home run! It landed in the right

Bo has spent a lot of his free time helping kids.

center-field bleachers. The blast was the longest hit at Yankee Stadium that year. Brian was awestruck.

Bo wasn't through. In the fifth inning, he came up for the third time. Brett and Kevin Seitzer were now on base. Bo didn't expect to see a good pitch. Hawkins had already been burned twice. There was no way he'd give Bo anything good to hit.

Hawkins threw a slider. Bo swung and lifted a fly ball to right field. It looked like an easy out. But then the ball kept going and going. It landed three rows back in the stands. It was another home run! Bo had come to bat three times and had hit three balls over the fence! He had driven in seven runs. Now Brian was really smiling.

Bo had a chance to make history. Only nine men had ever hit four home runs in a game. No one had ever hit five. Bo had already given Brian Newton the night of his life. Could he enter baseball's record books that night, too?

The answer was no. Bo didn't get a chance to bat again. In the bottom of the sixth inning, he tried to make a diving catch in the outfield. Bo landed awkwardly and injured his shoulder. He had to come out of the game. He was placed on the disabled list the following day and missed 30 days of play.

Bo is now 33 years old. In April 1995, he announced his retirement from baseball. Bo said that he is interested in an acting career. Whatever happens, his place in history is secure. Bo became one of the very best players in both baseball and football. His success paved the way for other two-sport stars like Deion Sanders. Sanders is the only athlete to play in both a World Series and a Super Bowl.

Will there be any more athletes like Bo and Deion? It's tough to say. Bo thinks it's very difficult to play two sports. Bodies need time to rest and recover. And baseball teams don't want their guys playing a rough sport like football.

Bo beat the odds in so many ways. He overcame a troubled youth. He earned very good money with his talent and hard work. He came back from a serious injury. Some have called it a miracle to be able to play baseball with an artificial hip.

Bo has given us some tremendous thrills. He will always be remembered as one of the greatest athletes of his time.

Bo Jackson's
Career Highlights

1982   Drafted by New York Yankees after senior year at McAdory High School. Declines contract offer and enrolls at Auburn University on a football scholarship.

1985   Wins Heisman Trophy as nation's top college football player. Becomes Auburn's all-time leading rusher (4,303 yards).

1986   Drafted first overall by NFL's Tampa Bay Buccaneers. Chosen in fourth round of baseball draft by Kansas City Royals. Signs contract with Royals.

1987   Announces he will play football after the baseball season ends. Joins the Los Angeles Raiders. Rushes for 221 yards on "Monday Night Football" against the Seattle Seahawks.

1989   Hits memorable home run in baseball's All-Star Game.

1990   Belts at least 20 homers for fourth consecutive season.

1991   Injures hip in football game. Released by Royals and signs with Chicago White Sox. Receives artificial hip in 1992 and vows to return to baseball.

1993   Hits home run in first at-bat of season. Named Comeback Player of the Year by *The Sporting News*.

1994   Signs with California Angels.

1995   Announces retirement from baseball, interest in spending more time with his family, and pursuing a movie career.

Bo Jackson's
Major League Baseball Statistics

Year	Team	Average	At-Bats	Hits	Home Runs	RBIs
1986	Royals	.207	82	17	2	9
1987	Royals	.235	396	93	22	53
1988	Royals	.246	439	108	25	68
1989	Royals	.256	515	132	32	105
1990	Royals	.272	405	110	28	78
1991	White Sox	.255	71	16	3	14
1992	Injured—did not play					
1993	White Sox	.232	284	66	16	45
1994	Angels	.279	201	56	13	43
Major League Totals		.250	2,393	598	141	415

Bo Jackson's
National Football League Statistics

Rushing					Receiving		
Year	Team	Carries	Yards	TDs	Catches	Yards	TDs
1987	Raiders	81	554	4	16	136	2
1988	Raiders	136	580	3	9	79	0
1989	Raiders	173	950	4	9	69	0
1990	Raiders	125	698	5	6	68	0
NFL Totals		515	2,782	16	40	352	2

Further Reading

Bloom, Marc. *Know Your Football Game.* New York:
  Scholastic, 1990.

Devaney, John. *Bo Jackson: A Star for All Seasons.*
  New York: Walker and Co., 1992.

Foley, Red. *Red Foley's Best Baseball Book.*
  New York: Simon & Schuster, 1994.

Gutman, Bill. *Football.* North Bellmore, New York:
  Marshall Cavendish, 1990.

Hollander, Zader. *The Baseball Book.* New York:
  Random House, 1991.

Rolfe, John. *Bo Jackson.* Minneapolis: Lerner, 1991.

———. *Bo Jackson.* New York: Little, 1991.

Rothaus, James R. *Bo Jackson.* Plymouth, MN,
  1991.

Thornley, Stew. *The First Book of Football.*
  Minneapolis: Lerner, 1993.

Index